I0176049

PROJECT NEBO
Empowering the Generations

Ashley Davis, Emily Kincaid,
and Geoffrey Lentz

New Fire Press
Pensacola, Florida
2025

Copyright © 2025, Geoffrey D. Lentz.
All Rights Reserved.

Unless otherwise marked, scripture quotations are taken from the New Revised Standard Version Updated Edition . Copyright © 2021 National Council of Churches of Christ in the United States of America. Used by permission. All rights reserved worldwide.

Cover Design: Jeb Eugene Hunt

ISBN: 978-1-63199-937-6
eISBN: 978-1-63199-938-

New Fire Press
6 East Wright Street
Pensacola, FL 32501

newfirepress.com

To the climbers of Nebo—

the saints who lead with strength

and let go with grace;

who stand on the heights and see the land

they will not enter.

To the ones who now cross over,

who are called to lead, bold and trembling.

And to the Lord who goes before,

whose promise endures through every generation.

Contents

INTRODUCTION	vii
ONE Going to Nebo: The Church in Crisis	1
TWO Team Moses: Preparing to Pass the Baton	15
THREE Team Joshua: Courage to Lead	27
FOUR Team Rahab: The Faith of Outsiders	39
FIVE Team Yahweh: The God Who Transforms	51
SIX Nebo's Blessing: Moving Forward to the Promise	65
APPENDIX A A Case Study: First United Methodist of Pensacola, Florida	75
APPENDIX B Using Project Nebo in a Local Church	79

BIBLIOGRAPHY	89
ABOUT THE AUTHORS	91
ABOUT THIS BOOK	93

Introduction

In the scriptural imagination, Nebo is a place of transition. On Mount Nebo, the Lord revealed the Promised Land to Moses and passed the leadership baton to Joshua—a symbolic transition from one generation to the next. In our contemporary context, the world faces a Nebo moment, characterized by a leadership crisis and the crucial handoff from one generation to another. Project Nebo is designed to help the church talk about the historical transition that is occurring and to help each generation discern what God is calling them to do in this season.

Sociologists William Strauss and Neil Howe's generational theory illuminates the paradigm shifts occurring across generations. The Western World is currently in a significant generational transition, called the "Fourth Turning," which is marked by challenges akin to historical upheavals such as the Industrial Revolution, the American Civil War, the Great Depression, and World War II. At the core of this transition lies the challenge of passing the baton to the next generation of leaders.

Presently, both society and the church focus on the issues of older generations, neglecting the challenges faced by the majority—particularly the Millennials, now the largest generation. The church has an imperative to pivot toward the future, involving and empowering this generation in leadership and planning. The time has come for a proactive approach, and thus, Project Nebo emerges as a pathway for local churches to address generational transitioning and call each generation to leadership. Such times call for a reevaluation of leadership, a reinvigoration of community engagement, and a renewed focus on passing the torch to the next generation with grace, intention, and strategic foresight.

Project Nebo is not just an analytical tool; it is a call to action. It seeks to engage all generations within the church in a dialogue about their roles and responsibilities in this era of change. By metaphorically taking congregants to Nebo, the project fosters a collective envisioning of the future, urging members to discern their calling through the guidance of the Holy Spirit. This initiative champions the idea that every generation has a unique contribution to make, acknowledging the strengths and addressing the concerns of each.

The project outlines three distinct teams: Team Moses, representing the wisdom and experience of older generations; Team Joshua, embodying the vigor and potential of younger generations poised to lead; and Team Rahab, highlighting the value of fresh perspectives brought by newcomers to the faith community. Each team plays a critical role in the church's journey towards a promising future, emphasizing collaboration, mutual respect, and shared vision.

To better envision this transformative journey, readers are invited to reflect on the biblical account of Moses and the transition to Joshua's leadership, drawing parallels to our current context. This story is not just an historical recount but a timeless lesson on leadership, faith, and the eternal cycle of renewal. The Old Testament narrative serves as a powerful reminder that every generation faces its Nebo moment—a time to look forward with hope, to trust in divine guidance, and to pass on the legacy of faith with courage and conviction.

Yet, the three teams do not walk alone. It is the presence of Almighty God who is calling the church forward to new places and to new life. While the statistics and headlines seem dire for the church in America, God is not through with it yet. Project Nebo calls on the church to trust the working of the Holy Spirit to lead us to a promised place.

In embarking on Project Nebo, may the church be inspired by the scriptural imagination that sees transitions not as endings but as opportunities for growth, empowerment, and revitalization. God's people can hold fast to the promise that, with God's guidance, every generational handoff can lead to a future filled with promise and purpose. Through this initiative, the covenant community aspires to not only navigate the challenges of the present age but to forge a path that honors the past, engages the present, and embraces the future with unwavering faith and collective vision.

ONE

Going to Nebo: The Church in Crisis

Deuteronomy 34

> *Then Moses went up from the plains of Moab to Mount Nebo, to the top of Pisgah, which is opposite Jericho, and the Lord showed him the whole land: Gilead as far as Dan, ²all Naphtali, the land of Ephraim and Manasseh, all the land of Judah as far as the Western Sea, ³the Negeb, and the Plain—that is, the valley of Jericho, the city of palm trees—as far as Zoar. ⁴The Lord said to him, 'This is the land of which I swore to Abraham, to Isaac, and to Jacob, saying, "I will give it to your descendants"; I have let you see it with your eyes, but you shall not cross over there.'*

The Current Crisis

There is a crisis in the American Church. In 2,000, 70 percent of people reported that they belonged to a church. Just twenty years later, prior to any influence from the COVID-19 pandemic, only 47 percent claimed to have a church family.[1] Authors of a new book called *Dechurched* say that in the last two decades more people have left the church than joined the church during the first great awakening, the second great awakening, and the Billy Graham crusades combined.[2] The world is witnessing the greatest change in the religious landscape in American history. The dynamic shift is accelerated because people are leaving the church who never would have thought of leaving the church in the past. Many people who grew up in the church or were an integral part of the life of the church, have left. The data says that this is true of people who say they are liberal and conservative. The church has lost connection with people from all walks of life. Right now there are over 20 million Americans (16 percent of the population) who previously attended church and now no longer do. These people have been labeled as "dechurched."[3]

---

1 Jones, Jeffrey M. "U.S. Church Membership Falls Below Majority for First Time." *Gallup News*, March 29, 2021.
2 Davis, Jim, Collin Hansen, Michael Graham, and Ryan P. Burge. *The Great Dechurching: Who's Leaving, Why Are They Going, and What Will It Take to Bring Them Back?* (Zondervan Reflective, 2023), 5.
3 Davis, Hansen, Graham, Burge, *The Great Dechurching*, 5.

The predominant factor giving rise to this crisis is a generational challenge. While the church has lost ground in every generation, its greatest challenge is with young people. The Millennial and Gen Z (also called Homeland) generations have seen the largest decline. Right now, Millennials are the largest generation in American society, and yet they constitute the smallest demographic in the church.

Strauss-Howe Generational Theory

Two writers and sociologists, William Strauss and Neil Howe developed a theory in the 1990s that helps explain some of these dynamics. This theory came into the mainstream with their second book in 1998 called *The Fourth Turning*.[4] In 2023, Howe continued their shared work after Strauss's death and released an updated volume titled *The Fourth Turning is Here* to address twenty-first century developments. The Strauss-Howe Generational Theory posits that societal cycles recur approximately every eighty to ninety years, which aligns with four generations. This cycle consists of four "turnings," each representing a distinct era with unique societal characteristics and moods. These turnings shape the attitudes, values, and behaviors of the generation. A brief description of each turning follows:

---

4 Howe, Neil, and William Strauss. *The Fourth Turning: An American Prophecy*. (Broadway Books, 1998).

- First Turning (High): A period of strong communal values, where society is focused on building organizations, processes, and institutions that lead to a strong social fabric.
- Second Turning (Awakening): A phase of spiritual revival and cultural change, often challenging established norms and institutions.
- Third Turning (Unraveling): Characterized by individualism and the decay of established social structures.
- Fourth Turning (Crisis): A time of significant upheaval and transformation, leading to the rebuilding of society's structures and values as the cycle begins anew.

Each of these turnings shape a generation in somewhat predictable patterns.[5] According to the theory, we are living in the "fourth turning."

The Baton

What the American public is witnessing in this fourth turning, like each of the fourth turnings before this, is a difficult handoff. Human civilization is like a relay race.

In the ancient world, the relay race was far more than an athletic competition—it was a vital method of communication across vast distances. This practice, which predates modern postal systems

---

[5] Howe, Neil. *The Fourth Turning Is Here: What the Seasons of History Tell Us about How and When This Crisis Will End.* (Simon & Schuster, 2023.)

and electronic communication, used swift-footed couriers to deliver messages, leveraging human endurance and speed to bridge the communication gaps between distant cities.

The baton in these ancient relays was not merely a stick passed from runner to runner; it was a vessel of crucial information. Sometimes, it was a simple tree branch, symbolizing specific news such as victory or truce. Other times, it carried more complex messages, including written notes or ciphered instructions on a strip of leather wound around the baton.

The most iconic story of such a courier is that of Pheidippides, whose primary role was to run long distances to deliver urgent news. After the Greeks achieved an improbable victory over the Persians at the Battle of Marathon, a strategic military and political communication was needed. Despite having already run approximately 150 miles in the days preceding, Pheidippides was tasked with the critical mission of announcing the Greek victory to Athens to prevent any demoralization that might be caused by Persian misinformation.

Carrying a laurel branch, traditionally a symbol of triumph, Pheidippides ran the approximately 26.2 miles from Marathon to Athens. Upon arrival, he delivered his message, "Joy, we won," before succumbing to exhaustion and dying. This dramatic moment underscored the profound physical and emotional toll of such a responsibility but also highlighted the critical importance of timely and reliable communication in shaping historical events.

This type of message of victory was considered "good news" or gospel. The term "gospel" originally entered the lexicon with a very practical and worldly meaning akin to the message delivered by Pheidippides. The term was used to describe the joyous tidings of a military victory or other significant civic event.

This historical usage enriches our understanding of the term as it transitioned into religious contexts, particularly within Christianity, to signify the "good news" of Jesus Christ's life, death, and resurrection. Just as Pheidippides delivered his message of victory, Christians are tasked with sharing the transformative message of Christ's victory over sin and death. However, unlike the solitary run of Pheidippides, this spiritual message is a collective relay; it is passed from believer to believer, each contributing to the ongoing spread of this vital message through time and across cultures.

Each generation is on the same team: each is called to run with the baton and to hand the baton successfully to those who come behind them. But the most important part of the relay race is the handoff. Both runners have to run in step—at the same pace— to complete the handoff. They have to work together for the sake of the team.

The Nebo Challenge

The people of God faced their own challenge in the end of the book of Deuteronomy. Moses, the great prophet, had led them out of slavery in Egypt. Before they could enter the Promised Land, they had to go through the wilderness. They wandered in the wilderness for forty years, over the Sinai peninsula, maybe into Arabia, and then into the area that is now called the country of Jordan.

Moses was a faithful prophet who led God's people out of slavery in Egypt. He had met God in the burning bush and on Mount Sinai. He led them through the Red Sea and the desolate wilderness. But there was more. His job was not finished. God's goal for Moses and the Hebrew children was not just freedom from slavery. God wanted to give them the Promised Land. God wanted them to have a place where they could prosper. Moses's biggest job was to prepare the people for God's promise, but the promise was so big that Moses would not live to see it completed. The reason why they left slavery in Egypt was to inherit the promise. Moses's most important duty was to raise up Joshua as the next leader for God's people. Moses is often celebrated for his role in parting the Red Sea and the miracles of the wilderness: manna, quail, water from the rock, and meeting with God to receive the Ten Commandments. But his most important duty was passing the mission on to the next generation.

Near the end of Moses's ministry God called him to empower Joshua to lead. When the Hebrew people gathered at the foot of Mount Nebo, God called Moses to bless them, to bless Joshua, and to remind them of the mission to pursue God's promise. God called Joshua to step up and be a leader. Moses and Joshua had a successful handoff of the leadership baton. Moses had been mentoring Joshua and preparing him for years, even decades, for this moment. Despite being of different generations, they were on the same team.

The Church as a Team

The church is such a team. For two thousand years, each generation has been handing off the good news of Jesus Christ to the ones who come behind. No one is called to complete the journey on his or her own. Collectively, each generation is called to steward the baton and move it forward. The goal is to pass on the mission for the next leg of the race. It is not about any one person or even one generation—it is about the baton. The baton must move forward. Each person has a role to play.

Each generation is called to lead in its own way. It must be noted that there is sensitivity around the naming of generations. Each generation is resistant to and uncomfortable with the stereotypes and characteristics that define it. Internet memes such as "OK Boomer" and "Snowflake" are good examples of this. Human beings are complicated. Some don't fit neatly in their generation, having an old soul or young heart. There are not good and bad generations. Each generation has something to offer.

In 1 Corinthians, St. Paul tells the church about this relay using an agricultural metaphor. He says,

"⁶I planted, Apollos watered, but God gave the growth. ⁷So neither the one who plants nor the one who waters is anything, but only God who gives the growth. ⁸The one who plants and the one who waters have a common purpose, and each will receive wages according to the labor of each. ⁹For we are God's servants, working together..."(1 Corinthians 3:6-9).

Across generations and leadership styles, the church as a whole has been entrusted with the single task of handing the good news of Jesus Christ to the next in line. Each is called to play a part—but it is God who moves the church on to victorious transformation in Jesus Christ.

The Handoff

It was noted earlier that the handoff is the most sensitive part of the race. Some wrongly assume that one runner runs to a point and stops before handing the baton to another runner. In reality, both runners run together for a segment. They keep pace together so that the baton never slows down. They run together side by side, until the transfer is complete. Even with the fastest and best runners, without a successful handoff, the team risks coming in last place.

God is calling the church to a successful handoff in this critical time. Older members are not being asked to step down. To the contrary, the church needs them to step up—to lead, and, like Moses, to see mentoring and empowering new leaders as the most important part of their job. Additionally, new leaders—Joshuas—are also called at this critical time to step up. God is calling the church to keep pace together and prepare for the handoff.

The Story of Woz

Andrew Root's book, *Churches and Crisis of Decline*, tells a fictional but true story about a young man named Woz.[6] Woz's grandmother went to church every time it was open. She was a pillar of the church. But Woz, a Millennial, did not go to church. He got into a bit of trouble and lost his way in life. But he loved his grandmother, who had told him repeatedly that if he ever found himself out of options and in despair to go to her church. The people there would help him. Eventually, his grandmother passed away and Woz found himself at a dead end. Having run out of options, he finally went to his grandmother's church and asked for someone to help him "find God." The church people were stunned. They had never had anyone do this before, and they were not prepared. He was the youngest person there. He dressed in a different way, he

---

6   Root, Andrew. *Churches and the Crisis of Decline: A Hopeful, Practical Ecclesiology for a Secular Age.* (Baker Academic, a division of Baker Publishing Group, 2022.)

had different views about things, but he wanted to "find God." The Sunday school class struggled to help him, and the pastor could not find the right words. They had forgotten how to make disciples. This story is emblematic of the challenging generational handoff the church is experiencing. Now is the time for the church to rediscover the joy of running the race so that new runners might be invited into that joy.[7]

What is the mission of the church? Why does the church exist? The church exists not for itself, but for the sake of the world.

All Are Called to Lead

God is calling each generation of the church to lead. As will be discussed in the following chapters, each character in the story represents a different segment of the church. Moseses, Joshuas, and Rahabs each have a role. God is calling all who follow Jesus to go like Moses up to the top of Nebo and see the promise, the future that God has in store. There, one generation prepares to pass the baton to the next.

---

7 "Therefore, since we are surrounded by so great a cloud of witnesses, let us also lay aside every weight and the sin that clings so closely, and let us run with perseverance the race that is set before us, looking to Jesus the pioneer and perfecter of our faith, who for the sake of the joy that was set before him endured the cross, disregarding its shame, and has taken his seat at the right hand of the throne of God.
Consider him who endured such hostility against himself from sinners, so that you may not grow weary or lose heart." Hebrews 12:1-3

In Dr. Martin Luther King's last speech, he was ensuring that the civil rights movement was being passed on to those who would come after him. As he spoke of the pursuit of God's promise, he referred to Mount Nebo. He said, "But it really doesn't matter with me now, because I've been to the mountaintop ... I've seen the Promised Land. I may not get there with you. But I want you to know tonight, that we, as a people, will get to the Promised Land."[8]

The church as the people of God will get to the Promised Land, not by its own strength, but by the God who delivered the Hebrews from slavery in Egypt. Each follower of Christ gets the opportunity to participate in God's salvation story. God is calling the church forward to go up to Nebo and get a vision for the future.

Prayer

God of Moses and Miriam, God of Joshua and Rahab, you who have been our dwelling place for all generations: Grant us, your people, the sheep of your own flock, the courage to hear your voice among the many noises that fill our ears, that, having heard your voice we would follow where you lead us.

We confess that we often forget that we were once outsiders, and that it is only by the grace of Jesus

---

[8] King, Martin Luther Jr. "I've Been to the Mountaintop." Audio recording, April 3, 1968, Memphis, Tennessee.

through the waters of our baptism that we have been incorporated into your mighty acts of salvation. Especially those of us who have long been church people forget that your church, your mission, does not belong to us. And yet through the mystery of your mercy, you have tasked us with stewarding your good news in the world.

On our own, we are lousy messengers, sometimes lazy, sometimes forgetful, sometimes selfish. But through the power of your Holy Spirit working in this beloved community, you grant us abilities we could never have on our own.

Remind us once again of the grace which calls us children of the most high God. Teach us to keep pace with you so that we may do what is ours to do in your divine economy. And make us ever ready to train up new leaders for your people, for the sake of your mission, so that all people may know their belovedness in your eyes.

In the name of the Father, and of the Son, and of the Holy Spirit. Amen.

TWO

Team Moses: Preparing to Pass the Baton

Deuteronomy 30: 5-6, 31:1-8

⁵The Lord your God will bring you into the land that your ancestors possessed, and you will possess it; he will make you more prosperous and numerous than your ancestors. 6 Moreover, the Lord your God will circumcise your heart and the heart of your descendants, so that you will love the Lord your God with all your heart and with all your soul, in order that you may live.

When Moses had finished speaking all these words to all Israel, he said to them: "I am now one hundred twenty years old. I am no longer able to get about, and the Lord has told me, 'You shall not cross over this Jordan.' The Lord your God himself will cross over before you. He will destroy these nations before you, and you shall dispossess them. Joshua also will cross over before you, as the Lord promised. The Lord will do to them as he did to Sihon and Og, the kings of the Amorites, and to their land, when he destroyed them. The Lord will give them over to you and you shall deal with them in full accord with the command that I have given to you. Be strong and bold; have no fear or dread of them, because it is the Lord your God who goes with you; he will not fail you or forsake you."Then Moses summoned Joshua and said to him in the sight of all Israel: "Be strong and bold, for you are the one who will go with this people into the land that the Lord has sworn to their ancestors to give them; and you will put them in possession of it. It is the Lord who goes before you. He will be with you; he will not fail you or forsake you. Do not fear or be dismayed."

Lost Language

There was a story published in the last couple of years about an 89 year-old-man named Blas Omar Jaime. He lives in Argentina and is a part of an indigenous people called the Chaná. This group of people made their living for over 2,000 years on the Parana River, the second largest in South America. While watching the news one day,

Jaime heard someone say that the Chaná language had become extinct. He responded, "I exist. I am here." He had been taught all his life to be silent, to not speak up for fear of persecution and to keep his language to himself. Realizing that he was the only speaker of his language remaining, he knew it was time to speak out. So he reached out to the folks at UNESCO, whose mission includes the preservation of languages. They report that 40 percent of the world's languages, more than 2,600, are in danger of going extinct. Jaime sat down with a linguist and produced a dictionary with over 1,000 words. He has taught the language to his daughter, Evangelina, who now teaches the Chaná language to young people so that the Chaná culture can be passed on. He says, "Language is what gives you identity. If someone doesn't have their language, they're not a people."[9]

Team Moses

Jaime's story is instructive for our older generations—those who are called Team Moses in this series. Within the senior ranks of most churches, there is a fountain of wisdom that has been passed down through ages. Part of this wisdom is the language of faith. Christians have a certain grammar—a unique way of talking about God, humanity, and world. Today, this language is also at risk of

---

[9] Alcoba, Natalie. "This Language Was Long Believed Extinct. Then One Man Spoke Up." Reporting from Paraná, Argentina, January 13, 2024.

extinction. This unique way of speaking and living could be lost if it is not passed down to the generations to come. Christianity is always only one generation away from extinction. That may sound too strong, but it is true. Jesus's plan for the world to know salvation is for the church to pass down the good news. Jesus chose twelve apostles, and they, in turn, handed the gospel on to others. For 2,000 years, generations have been passing down the faith.

The church is currently in a crisis period, facing a difficult handoff of the good news from one generation to the next. There is a unique or special calling by God for older members of churches. They have so much experience and wisdom, and the church needs that now more than ever. The great thing about seniors these days is that they are younger than ever. Today's seniors of all ages are filled with energy and vitality. There has never been a generation that has been so age-defying. Today's seniors refuse to slow down; they are the backbone of the church in America and the foundation of modern society.

There is a Native American phrase that says, "No wise person ever wanted to be younger." Aging comes with a lot of benefits. As you grow older, a person comes to know himself or herself and to find his or her life's purpose. David Brooks, author and social commentator, in his book, The Second Mountain, describes aging using the image of mountain trekking life's second mountain. It goes along with our theme of climbing Mount Nebo perfectly. He says,

> You don't climb the second mountain the way you climb the first mountain. You conquer your first mountain. You identify the summit, and you claw your way toward it. You are conquered by your second mountain. You surrender to some summons, and you do everything necessary to answer the call and address the problem or injustice that is in front of you. On the first mountain you tend to be ambitious, strategic, and independent. On the second mountain you tend to be relational, intimate, and relentless.[10]

He goes on to say,

> If the first mountain is about building up the ego and defining the self, the second mountain is about shedding the ego and losing the self. If the first mountain is about acquisition, the second mountain is about contribution.[11]

---

10 Brooks, David. *The Second Mountain: The Quest for a Moral life*. (Penguin Books, 2020), xvi.
11 Ibid.

Our older members have faced so many challenges and have learned the ultimate emptiness of success and achievement. The wise ones have turned outward and upward in serving God and neighbor.

Moses and Joshua

This is what Moses did. He had seen a lot. He was born in Egypt and floated down the Nile as an infant. He had seen the inside of Pharaoh's palace, but he also saw the poverty of slavery outside the palace walls. He had a foot in both realities. He had seen the burning bush ablaze and heard the voice of God. He led God's people faithfully from Egypt through the plagues and sea. He was a wildly successful leader, but it never was supposed to be about Moses.

Moses's most important duty was to prepare the next generation to inherit the Promised Land. He chose Joshua to be the next leader. Exodus 24 states, "So Moses set out with his assistant Joshua, and Moses went up into the mountain of God." Joshua was there on Mount Sinai when Moses communed with God and received the Ten Commandments. He is not mentioned at all in that part of the story, but sure enough, when Moses comes down from the mountain in 32:17, Joshua is mentioned again—he was with Moses the whole time.

Why did Moses take Joshua up Mount Sinai to meet with God? It's likely that he was mentoring him. Sinai is the place where God met with the people,and Moses made sure that young Joshua was there with him to know firsthand the presence of God and the importance of the covenant. The handoff did not start at MountNebo-but at Mount Sinai. Moses made sure that Johua had a firsthand relationship with God. Leading God's people is not primarily about being a good speaker. Moses was not. It is not being a great person. Moses struggled with significant ethical challenges, including a time when he committed murder. Leading God's people starts with a relationship with God, and that is what Moses handed on to Joshua. When the time for the Nebo Project had come and it was time for Joshua to lead, he was ready. Moses had prepared him, given him room to grow in his faith, to make mistakes, and to be a part of Moses's larger leadership team.

The care and intention in Moses's leadership style is especially apparent when compared to that of his older brother Aaron. Moses and Aaron were of the same generation, but they viewed their plight and purpose very differently. Some of the Israelites who had Aaron's ear did not share Moses's desire to follow God's will. Complaining loudly, they formed a rather influential back-to-Egypt committee. They wanted to return to slavery because in Egypt they at least had meat and melons. It's been said that the last seven words of a church are, "We have never done it that way before." These disgruntled Israelites could not handle the wildness and unpredictability of God's redemption.

While Moses and Joshua were up on the mountain, the people clamored for gods made with human hands, and Aaron made for them a golden calf. Instead of worshiping the wild God who leads God's people through the wilderness, they chose a domesticated deity that they could control and move around. A god that would follow them all the way back to Egypt instead of leading them to freedom and salvation.

God's people today have that same choice. The church can be like Moses and worship the God who cannot be controlled. The outcome cannot be known, and this God will lead the church to a place that it has never been. This journey will be difficult, and it will be costly. It will require everything and more, but it will lead to life. Alternatively, the church can choose the way of Aaron and the others and worship a much smaller deity that agrees with the status quo. That deity does not challenge the deeply held traditions and follows the people wherever *they* want to go. The church today has a choice to make. Moses, in Deuteronomy 30:19b, at the foot of Mount Nebo, lays this choice out before the people, saying,"I have set before you life and death, blessings and curses. Choose life so that you and your descendants may live..."

Neil Howe, in his book, *The Fourth Turning is Here*, says that the older generations have this same choice: "It is easy to envision [Baby Boomers] as pillars of fire leading to the Promised Land—but just as easy to see them as unhinged Ahabs determined to wreck the ship and take everyone down with them. Either is possible."[12]

God is calling for the Moseses to take younger and more inexperienced members up Sinai to talk openly about the faith and make sure that the younger and new members are connecting with God and are a part of the covenant. Some members of these older generations say that they have given up on Millennials or Gen Zs. They do not believe that the younger generations have the capacity to carry it forward. The truth is that the church does not have the luxury of being able to give up on any generation. God's people have to trust, if not younger generations, then God's Holy Spirit to move the church forward through the ages.

Ultimately, the choice at Nebo and its promise is not just for the older generations. While they are at a point in life where they can hear the promise most clearly and make the choice, each generation is called to the same task. All are called to be ready to hand down what they have received to those who come after them. Even the infants in the church nursery are here to pass it on. All are Team Moses.

12   Howe, *The Fourth Turning is Here*, 348.

Baton Relay

The church is in a relay race that began long before this present age and will end long after current members and clergy are gone. In a relay, it is the duty of the runner with the baton to place it in the next runner's hand! The task of the handoff falls to the first runner. Moses did not wait for Joshua to take leadership, instead Moses put it in his hands.

So what is it that the church gets to pass on? What is the baton? There are many things that could be passed down—our traditions, values, principles. The church has a lot of traditions to pass on, and those who come after us will change some things and preserve others. Each generation tends to view the world a little differently from the ones who came before it. Each generation has to prioritize and be clear about what is handed down. The Greek word used in the New Testament for tradition is *paradidomi*. It means to hand down or hand off like in a relay race. What is the tradition to be handed down? The theologian Yaroslav Pelikan, taught that there is a difference between Tradition and Traditionalism. He said, "Tradition is the living faith of the dead. Traditionalism is the dead faith of living. "[13] Each generation of leaders of the church does not need to expect the next generation to do church in the exact same way, but to find the core,

---

[13] The Vindication of Tradition: 1983 Jefferson Lecture in the Humanities (1984), p.65

the most important part. This is where St. Paul helps us in 1 Corinthian 15:1-3.

> Now I should remind you, brothers and sisters, of the good news that I proclaimed to you, which you in turn received, in which also you stand, through which also you are being saved...For I handed on to you as of first importance what I in turn had received: that Christ died for our sins in accordance with the scriptures,and that he was buried, and that he was raised on the third day...

Here Paul tells the church at Corinth that the core of the tradition is the good news of Jesus Christ. This includes Jesus's death and resurrection for the salvation of the world. This is of "first importance," he says. In fact, Paul says that this is the only thing that he handed on to them. Nothing else matters. Everything else is considered nothing compared to the good news of Jesus Christ and his grace.

It is crucial that the church be focused on passing down the most important part of what it means to be followers of Jesus. Maybe some of the other things will go along with it. But what must be passed down is a community that holds the cross at its center and the resurrection as its animating force. The church must proclaim the saving love of Jesus Christ.

Prayer

O God, you have been our help in ages past. You have been the faithful One in good times and in bad. Your presence has been the rock of our salvation. You have parted the seas, making a way when we couldn't see any way forward. You have led us from captivity to sin and the forces of death and have led us into the light of your presence.

We, on the other hand, have not been so faithful. We have longed for the certainty we knew when we were captives, preferring the temptations and proscribed nature of our old life to the freedom and wonder of the new life you offer. We would often rather eat the meat of our captors than the bread of heaven, which you feed us in those in-between places of wilderness and wandering.

Remind us once again that you are enough. Teach us to trust you with all our days, so that we may choose life and enjoy your abundance. Like Moses, when our days are ended, may we lie down and die at peace, trusting that you are the One in whom all things are held together.

Grant us the courage to do what is ours to do and to trust that you empower others to do their part as well. Teach us to run the race with confidence, to look toward the promised land, to train up new leaders to carry your good news, and to let go of the baton when our race has been completed.

In the name of the Father, and of the Son, and of the Holy Spirit. Amen.

THREE

Team Joshua: Courage to Lead

Joshua 1:1-9

After the death of Moses the servant of the Lord, the Lord spoke to Joshua son of Nun, Moses' assistant, saying, ²'My servant Moses is dead. Now proceed to cross the Jordan, you and all this people, into the land that I am giving to them, to the Israelites. ³Every place that the sole of your foot will tread upon I have given to you, as I promised to Moses. ⁴From the wilderness and the Lebanon as far as the great river, the river Euphrates, all the land of the Hittites, to the Great Sea in the west shall be your territory. ⁵No one shall be able to stand against you all the days of your life. As I was with Moses, so I will be with you; I will not fail you or forsake you. ⁶Be strong and courageous; for you shall put this people in possession of the land that I swore to their ancestors to give them. ⁷Only be strong and very courageous, being careful to act in accordance with all the law that my servant Moses commanded you; do not turn from it to the right hand or to the left, so that you may be successful wherever you go. ⁸This book of the law shall not depart out of your mouth; you shall meditate on it day and night, so that you may be careful to act in accordance with all that is written in it. For then you shall make your way prosperous, and then you shall be successful. ⁹I hereby command you: Be strong and courageous; do not be frightened or dismayed, for the LORD your God is with you wherever you go.'

Called to Lead

In the year 595 CE, a young man, almost a boy, was chosen by his bishop to be a missionary to what they believed were the most violent and pagan people. The bishop's name was Pope Gregory the Great, the young monk was later known as St. Augustine of Canterbury, and the violent and pagan people were the British-Anglo Saxon. When they got across the channel they looked and saw fortifications and strong warriors, and they did what anyone would do—they turned around. Augustine went back and told Gregory that the mission was not wise. But Gregory forced him to find the courage to go back over there and preach the gospel to them, and preach he did. He converted the heathens and became the Apostle to the English. He stepped up and became the leader that he was called to be.

Leadership Vacuum

There is a real leadership vacuum in the world right now. To some extent, the lack of leadership is understandable. The anti-institutionalist nature of the current "fourth turning" crisis period has caused people to be critical of any leader who stands up to lead. Furthermore, there is little clarity on how to move forward. Leadership has been crumbling in the nation and in the church for years. What the world needs now is good leaders. This, of course, is true for every generation. Older generations are needed to step up and to mentor and lead by example and character. Younger generations are also called to step up at a time like this. There are many valid reasons to sit on the sidelines. Some younger people don't feel they are allowed to lead or haven't been given the room to lead. Leaders of all ages feel like they are not prepared or not equipped to face the challenges of today. The story of Joshua, a man who was called to lead his people at a time of immense uncertainty, has long inspired leaders through the ages.

Joshua

Every time Joshua appears in scripture, there is a phrase that goes with him: "Be strong and courageous." That is what Moses tells Joshua when he is chosen. And that is what Moses tells him when he is commissioned to lead God's people. This is what God tells him to say to the people when he is their leader, and it is what he says to them. This is his motto—almost his mantra. Be strong and courageous! Do you know why that message was hammered into him at this time? Well, it must have been that he was prone to being afraid!

In Numbers 13, Joshua had been sent out with twelve spies to take a look at the Promised Land. When they arrived, they discovered that it was a real mess. There were already people living there and those people had built fortifications. It is hard to know exactly what they saw, but it was overwhelming. It was not the Promised Land that they had imagined. They were devastated. Ten of the spies came back saying that there were giants. These ten reported that the people who lived in the land were huge and could not be defeated. Maybe that was Joshua's take on it too. But then Caleb said, "We should go up and take possession of the land, for we can certainly do it." Caleb's proclamation was a pivotal moment in the history of the Israelites. Would they enter the Promised Land and trust God to help them make their home there or give in to fear and fail to act? Joshua joined Caleb and exhorted the people not to trust their own strength or power, but to trust the Lord. Of course, the ten spies prevailed and Caleb and Joshua lost the day. The people did not enter the Promised Land because they did not yet trust the Lord to make a home for them in the "land flowing with milk and honey." They spent the next 40 years wandering in the wilderness waiting for a new generation. The people were not ready, but in that moment Joshua found his strength and courage. And that call to "be strong and courageous" would carry him through the rest of his life.

Leading in a Time of Crisis

At the end of the Book of Deuteronomy, Joshua faced his biggest challenge. God had called him to lead the people into the Promised Land. They had wandered for forty years and not made any progress. It is hard to understate their weakness. It is easy to think of the Hebrews as a tribe of warriors, but that was not reality. They were a group of refugees that had just fled slavery. They had almost nothing. They didn't even have food except for what the Lord provided. They were refugees who had been camping out in the wilderness for a generation. One thing is clear: these people were not prepared to fight giants. They were not prepared to fight anyone. They were poor, unarmed, and ill prepared for battle, but the Lord told Moses it was time for the people to find their promised home. Moses laid his hands on Joshua and commissioned him to lead the people forward into the future. The words that Moses spoke to him were "Be strong and courageous."

This is the nature of passing the baton. Joshua's task was to pick up where Moses left off. The saints of the church have faithfully handed down the faith and traditions of the church until today. The church of today is called to take up the mantle of leadership from those who have come before.

In 2 Timothy 1, Paul tells Timothy, whom he is mentoring in the faith:

[5]I am reminded of your sincere faith, a faith that lived first in your grandmother Lois and your mother Eunice and now, I am sure, lives in you. [6]For this reason I remind you to rekindle the gift of God that is within you through the laying on of my hands; [7]for God did not give us a spirit of cowardice, but rather a spirit of power and of love and of self-discipline.

Here Paul talks about faith as spiritual DNA. He says that Timothy's faith was first in his grandmother and then in his mother and now has been passed to him. This faith was there but needs to be stirred up, its flames fanned. It is amazing to think of the mothers and fathers and their strong faith in previous generations. Their faith lives on in those who lead the church today.

Laying on of Hands

In the United Methodist tradition, at ordination the bishop lays hands on the ordinand and says, "take thou authority." The Bishop then gives a certificate of ordination and a list that some would call Apostolic Succession. In the ordination class of 2024 in the Alabama-West Florida Conference, the certificate shows seven sets of hands linking back to John Wesley. Then twenty-one hands back from him is St. Augustine of Canterbury. Then further back was St. Anselm, St. Irenaeus, St. Peter, and in 100 more hands you end up in the hands of Jesus. That shows an unbroken line of faith passed down from one generation to another. The faith of all those saints, of 2,000 years of Christian tradition lives in the church today. It is not about the gifts of a particular pastor or knowledge of the faith. The wisdom of the ages lives in each generation. Each time a pastor lays hands on the confirmands, she is passing that wisdom on to the young people with the trust that the faith will live on in them. Tradition means handing on the faith that one has received from those who have come before.

All followers of Jesus are heirs to a strong faith that has been passed down these 2,000 years. Now it is the day to carry forward the good news. The church faces some major challenges that are unlike what previous generations faced, but their wisdom lives on. God is searching for people to step forward and lead, especially younger people. Many of these people may not feel that they are adequately prepared. But just as God did with Moses, he is raising up leaders to be strong and courageous—even when they lack knowledge, skill, time, money, or other resources.

Jericho Strategy

Despite being mentored by Moses himself, Joshua lacked the resources and knowledge to lead the people to their promised home. He was not prepared, but he pressed on in strength and courage anyway. The old spiritual goes, "Joshua fit the battle of Jericho and the walls came tumbling down." Of course, that's not quite how it went. The Israelites were outnumbered and outgunned. They did not overcome Jericho by their military prowess or their superior force. Joshua did not fight the battle. It was God who did the work for them. All the Israelites had to do was march in circles, blow their horns, and the walls came tumbling down. Joshua is not known for his superior strength but for his trust in God. He believed that God would go before him and make a way. What Moses passed to Joshua was not a battle plan or a stockpile of munitions. It was faith.

Faith is all we need. The courage is not in ourselves but in God. God has called today's church leaders to lead through a crisis, through "the fourth turning." The current task is a successful handoff of the faith to the next generation, and there are a lot of challenges that make this difficult. During the Project Nebo sermon series at First UMC Pensacola, someone asked, "How is this going to work? What is the outcome for Project Nebo?" The answer is there is no set outcome. Today's church leaders are called to help everyone climb Mount Nebo and look into the future. They are called to faithfully bring together people of different generations to have this conversation illuminated by Scripture, and God will do the rest. This is the Jericho strategy. God's people are not called to tear down the walls and fight to victory. All that God has called church leaders to do is to step out in faith and lead—just to blow the horn. It is not about power but faith.

The Lord's Promise

The promise that the Lord gave Joshua is that, "As I was with Moses so I will be with you." Isn't that a great promise? As God was with those who came before, who carried the baton faithfully, so God will be with each generation. The church has all that it needs. There is a scene in Scripture when Joshua gets them to move forward and they are ready to enter the Promised Land. They faced an obstacle, the River Jordan, but when they stepped in, the waters parted, and they walked across dry land. The Jordan is not a big river, so it probably didn't need to be parted. The people probably could have waded through it. So why did God part the river? Maybe God performed the miracle because of his promise, "As I was with Moses so I will be with you." The God who delivered the Hebrews from slavery and parted the sea for Moses also parted the river for Joshua.

It is no wonder that when it was time to name the baby born in Bethlehem, the name the angel told Joseph to give to the child was Joshua. That was Jesus's name in Hebrew. Jesus is the one who is strong and courageous. He is the one who is leading the church forward. Between polarized politics at every level and wars in many places, this is an age of anxiety. But the church is called to be strong and courageous, not like the spies, but like Joshua. God's reality is not about the facts on the ground but about faith. God is calling leaders of all ages to take up the baton and run with it. It is time to be "strong and courageous."

Prayer

Almighty and everlasting God, you inhabit eternity and cannot be contained by time and space. And yet you have been with us since the beginning of time, guiding us, loving us, disciplining us, saving us. You are already in the future, making a way for the salvation of those who haven't even been born yet. You are a mystery to us. Your omnipresence baffles our human minds.

Like you did with Joshua, you encourage us to be strong and courageous, no matter what we may face in the coming days, weeks, months, and years, not because we are able but because you are. Like Joshua and David and so many other faithful followers, teach us to do the next right thing, leading when we are called to do so, even when you call us to march in circles or face giants with no armor or just look ridiculous by human standards.

Remind us that you will fight our battles for us if we will only be still and wait for you. May we be people who trust you with our very lives, who show the fruit of your spirit when it makes absolutely no worldly sense to do so. Sanctify us by your Holy Spirit and form us into your people who are known by your love, joy, peace, patience, kindness, gentleness, faithfulness, and self-control.

In the name of the Father, and of the Son, and of the Holy Spirit. Amen.

FOUR

Team Rahab:
The Faith of Outsiders

Joshua 2:1-24

>*Then Joshua son of Nun sent two men secretly from Shittim as spies, saying, 'Go, view the land, especially Jericho.' So they went, and entered the house of a prostitute whose name was Rahab, and spent the night there. ²The king of Jericho was told, 'Some Israelites have come here tonight to search out the land.' ³Then the king of Jericho sent orders to Rahab, 'Bring out the men who have come to you, who entered your house, for they have come only to search out the whole land.' ⁴But the woman took the two men and hid them. Then she said, 'True, the men came to me, but*

I did not know where they came from. ⁵And when it was time to close the gate at dark, the men went out. Where the men went I do not know. Pursue them quickly, for you can overtake them.' ⁶She had, however, brought them up to the roof and hidden them with the stalks of flax that she had laid out on the roof. ⁷So the men pursued them on the way to the Jordan as far as the fords. As soon as the pursuers had gone out, the gate was shut.

*8 Before they went to sleep, she came up to them on the roof ⁹and said to the men: 'I know that the L*ORD *has given you the land, and that dread of you has fallen on us, and that all the inhabitants of the land melt in fear before you. ¹⁰For we have heard how the L*ORD *dried up the water of the Red Sea* before you when you came out of Egypt, and what you did to the two kings of the Amorites that were beyond the Jordan, to Sihon and Og, whom you utterly destroyed. ¹¹As soon as we heard it, our hearts failed, and there was no courage left in any of us because of you. The L*ORD *your God is indeed God in heaven above and on earth below. ¹²Now then, since I have dealt kindly with you, swear to me by the L*ORD *that you in turn will deal kindly with my family. Give me a sign of good faith ¹³that you will spare my father and mother, my brothers and sisters, and all who belong to them, and deliver our lives from death.' ¹⁴The men said* *to her, 'Our life for yours! If you do not tell this business of ours, then we will deal kindly and faithfully with you when the Lord gives us the land.'*

15 Then she let them down by a rope through the window, for her house was on the outer side of the city wall and she resided within the wall itself. ¹⁶She said to them, 'Go towards the hill country, so that the pursuers may not come upon you. Hide yourselves there for three days, until the pursuers have returned; then afterwards you may go on your way.' ¹⁷The men said to her, 'We will be released from this oath that you have made us swear to you ¹⁸if we invade the land and you do not tie this crimson cord in the window through which you let us down, and you do not gather into your house your father and mother, your brothers, and all your family. ¹⁹If any of you go out of the doors of your house into the street, they shall be responsible for their own death, and we shall be innocent; but if a hand is laid upon any who are with you in the house, we shall bear the responsibility for their death. ²⁰But if you tell this business of ours, then we shall be released from this oath that you made us swear to you.' ²¹She said, 'According to your words, so be it.' She sent them away and they departed. Then she tied the crimson cord in the window.

Playing Keep-Away

The baton of the faith has been passed down from generation to generation. Moses passed it to Joshua, and it has been passed from leader to leader. But this is not the whole story. God finds leaders in unexpected places, and the most unexpected people become the center of God's story.

In history, oftentimes the baton of faith is seen as a ball of power in a game that is not fair. Often the powerful—the men, the rich, and the insiders—have tried to monopolize the baton. The people of God have been playing a game of keep-away. The boys have tried to keep it away from the girls. Certain races, religions, and backgrounds have tried to keep the baton away from other races, religions, and backgrounds. In some cases, the church has sought to protect or defend the baton instead of passing it on. When that happens, we are seeing the baton not as the good news of Jesus Christ but as a king's royal scepter or bishop's mighty crozier, a tool of power rather than service. The story of God's people is a human story and is often told from this perspective, but it is also God's story that is filled with surprises by radically including those we leave out.

Rahab

This is where the story of Rahab comes in. The story of Moses and Joshua leading the people into the Promised Land cannot be told without Rahab.

She may seem like a minor character, but her presence in the story is crucial. Usually, the church expects the mighty men of Israel to be the heroes, but in this first and most crucial challenge, it was Rahab. She was not an Israelite; she was a Canaanite from Jericho. She was an outsider, and she was a woman. Scholars suggest that she and her whole family were in abject poverty, likely in deep debt. They lived in a rich and powerful city, but they were barely getting by, and Rahab had resorted to prostitution to help feed her family. She was a strong woman who was taking care of everyone in her life. For some reason, the whole burden of her family was on her, and she did what was necessary to survive. Rahab made a deal with the enemy spies. She saw the writing on the wall, and she believed that the God of the Israelites would prevail. In fact, this outsider woman had more faith than most of the insiders of Israel. At great risk to herself, she hid the spies on her roof among stalks of flax and helped them down the wall with her crimson cord, becoming a savior not only to her family but to all of Israel.

It is a remarkable story that turns upside down much of what modern readers have come to expect. The least likely person saves the day for Israel. What is expected is for the Israelites to beat the Canaanites. The Deuteronomistic laws make it clear that the Israelites were to keep their distance from the Canaanites, But, here at the start of the story, all of that is deconstructed like the walls of

Jericho itself. Any notion of who is in and who is out "comes a-tumbling down." Rahab the Harlot, a Canaanite woman, was brought into Israel with her whole family. In the New Testament, Rahab is praised for her faith in that famous passage in Hebrews 11: 31, where all the giants of the faith are listed. Then in James 2:25, she is praised for putting her faith into action with good works. In the New Testament, Rahab is an example of how a Christian should live. The woman who was an outsider is moved to the center of God's story.

The Passover Covenant

In the Book of Joshua, there are some subtle hints that show us how Rahab, who should have been outside the covenant and outside the faith, was brought into it. First, she hid the spies in flax. That detail is significant because the flax harvest was a sign that it was time for Passover, indicating that this story is a Passover story. Second and most dramatically, Rahab was to display a crimson rope in her window as a sign of salvation, echoing how the Israelites marked their doors with crimson blood during the Exodus. The crimson rope was a sign that God brought Rahab into the Passover covenant—she became part of the people of God.

Jesus's Family Tree

The most remarkable thing about Rahab is her family, specifically, her descendants. The Gospel of Matthew begins with the most unusual family tree.

The Bible is filled with family trees, also known as the begats. Most people usually skip over the begats when reading scripture. The begats don't make it into the lectionary. They can be tedious—so-and-so begat so-and-so begat so-and-so. And in many ways Jesus's lineage seems like that typical Biblical family tree. It starts with "Abraham, the father of Isaac, the father of Jacob." Jesus's lineage is really a who's who of the Bible: Boaz, the father of Obed, Obed the father of Jesse, Jesse the father of King David, David the father of Solomon. This is quite a pedigree. But then this family tree starts throwing curve balls, and it is not boring at all—it is down right scandalous. Boaz's father was Salman and Boaz's mother was Rahab. This is the list of the matriarchs and patriarchs, and there in the line is Rahab. Neither Moses or Joshua are patriarchs here. Instead, the name lifted from this period of Biblical history is Rahab. She becomes the really-great grandmother of David. Not only does it mention Rahab as David's grandmother but it also lists a few more surprising names—Tamar, Ruth, and Bathsheba. There are four women mentioned in this holy genealogy—the royal family tree of Israel, and they are all gentiles. They are all outsiders, and they are matriarchs. And this is not just King David's family tree, this is Jesuss' family tree. These are Jesus's people.

This genealogy may appear, at first glance, to show that the baton was mainly handed down from Moseses to Joshuas, but that story is incomplete. The baton was also passed down from the Tamars, the Rahabs, the Ruths, and the Bathshebas. They were not born into the family, but God brought them in and gave them a place. They carried the baton, and they faithfully passed it down to us. There are countless others, women and men, people of different races and religions that God has used to carry and pass the baton. Moses would not have been anywhere without his sister Miriam, who helped him from the start and is a co-liberator of the Exodus according to Micah 6:4. The Bible refuses to tell the story with just the powerful and the mighty, instead it lifts up the lowly: the voices of women, immigrants, outsiders, and the poor. This is their story too. In Jesus Christ, everyone is brought into God's family. In Galatians 3:28-29, Paul states, "There is no longer Jew or Greek, there is no longer slave or free, there is no longer male and female; for all of you are one in Christ Jesus. [29]And if you belong to Christ, then you are Abraham's offspring, heirs according to the promise." The promises of the patriarchs and matriarchs are ours.

Reaching Nebo's Summit

The summit of Nebo is a place where God's people look to God's future and also pause and celebrate the Rahabs. Project Nebo is about giving thanks for new members and Rahabs who are joining the church while also giving thanks for the faithfulness of those who have been long-time members. Unfortunately, the church is one of the least diverse places in American society. For some reason, the church has often tried to find people who are just like those who are already in the pews, instead of following the Holy Spirit. When people from different races and places and different backgrounds and walks of life join a community, that community becomes richer and deeper. The valley of promise to which God is calling the church, flowing with milk and honey, will be built not on today's insiders but on today's outsiders who are just coming to faith. God is bringing them front and center.

Often, new members and visitors are excited about the church—they can imagine its future. They are ready to follow where God leads. Seeing the church through their eyes helps insiders see the future more clearly. Long-time church members take much for granted, thinking that things have to be a certain way and have certain limitations. But outsiders see possibilities everywhere. They can help open up the church to all of God's possibilities.

Gentile Inclusion

It is true that the people of God have often tried to play an elaborate game of keep-away with the baton, but it did not work. God brought so many people in despite God's people's hesitancy and fear. This is especially true in the Book of Acts. In the Pentecost event, we see the Holy Spirit including people from all over the world, "Parthinians, Medes, residents from Mesopotamia." On that day, the church was opened to everyone. The work of the Holy Spirit brings outsiders into the center. The first convert from Africa is the Ethiopian Eunuch, and he becomes a grandfather to the church today. The first convert in Europe is a woman named Lydia, who is the head of her own household and has her own business dying things purple—she is the church's grandmother. The Book of Acts is the story of God taking outsiders and placing them in the center and building the future on them.

That is what the church is. Gentiles, non-Jews, were all outsiders. By God's great gift in Jesus Christ, gentiles, like almost all members of the church today, have been brought into God's family. As 1 Peter 2:10 says, "Once you were not a people, but now you are God's people; once you had not received mercy, but now you have received mercy." In a sense, all people are Rahabs that God, in God's mercy, has brought into God's family. All insiders were once outsiders to God, and through esus Christ, all are invited to be part of God's family. As Jesus's great grandmother, the outsider Rahab is now the grandmother of the church. By hanging the crimson cord, she paved the way for all outsiders to have a place in God's story.

Peter says at Pentecost that this is all in fulfillment of what the prophet Joel spoke:

In the last days it will be, God declares, that I will pour out my Spirit upon all flesh, and your sons and your daughters shall prophesy, and your young men shall see visions, and your old men shall dream dreams. ...Then everyone who calls on the name of the Lord shall be saved.

The gift of the Holy Spirit is for all flesh. Yes, the church has had a hard time catching up to the Holy Spirit. Many groups of people have been and are excluded from leadership in most Christian groups, including women, African-Americans, and LGBTQ persons. Despite the fact that all were outsiders brought in like Rahab, there is often a lack of awareness of this fact and also a surprising hesitation to accept others. But in the gift of the Holy Spirit, the church has been gifted one another. Peter's proclamation from Joel is a sign that despite the church's dark past—it is time for men and women, old and young, and people from every race and ethnic group to take the baton. The Holy Spirit is bringing outsiders to the center and encouraging those who are uncertain of their place that they have a place. In fact, God is birthing the future of the church through the current outsiders just as he did through Rahab. God's plan to include Rahab and her family did not exclude Joshua and his family. Instead, as each outsider enters the family, he or she is woven into the fabric of God's people, making it even more beautiful than before. Current insiders of the church are not meant to play keep-away from outsiders or to feel threatened by new people. The church is called to pass the baton and welcome others into God's family so all can reach God's promised land together.

As the chorus of the African American spiritual "On Jordan's Stormy Banks I Stand" says, "I'm bound for the Promised Land. I bound for the Promised Land. Who will come and go with me, I'm bound for the Promised Land."

Prayer

God or every nation, tribe, and tongue, you welcome all people into your loving embrace.

Remind us that we were once far away from you. And that by the mystery of your mercy you now call us sons and daughters. Grant that we, your people, having been welcomed at your table, would be willing to welcome the outsider and to be changed by having welcomed them. Make us into your beloved community, a people who always make more room at the table.

In the story of Rahab, you teach us that your prevenient grace works in every person's heart before we have any knowledge of your mercy. May we accept your unconditional love so that we might be signposts of your hope, pointing always to you.

Grant us your peace as we look for your image in every face we meet.

In the name of the Father, and of the Son, and of the Holy Spirit. Amen.

FIVE

Team Y-h-w-h: The God Who Transforms

Exodus 3:1-8a

Moses was keeping the flock of his father-in-law Jethro, the priest of Midian; he led his flock beyond the wilderness, and came to Horeb, the mountain of God. ²There the angel of the Lord appeared to him in a flame of fire out of a bush; he looked, and the bush was blazing, yet it was not consumed. ³Then Moses said, 'I must turn aside and look at this great sight, and see why the bush is not burned up.' ⁴When the Lord saw that he had turned aside to see, God called to him out of the bush, 'Moses, Moses!' And he said, 'Here I am.' ⁵Then he said, 'Come no closer! Remove the sandals from your feet, for the place on which you are standing is holy ground.' ⁶He said further, 'I am the God of your father, the God of Abraham, the God of Isaac, and the God of Jacob.' And Moses hid his face, for he was afraid to look at God.

7 Then the Lord said, 'I have observed the misery of my people who are in Egypt; I have heard their cry on account of their taskmasters. Indeed, I know their sufferings, ⁸and I have come down to deliver them from the Egyptians, and to bring them up out of that land to a good and broad land, a land flowing with milk and honey.

Now What?

So far, this book has explored three teams trekking up the mountain: Teams Moses, Joshua, and Rahab. All three groups have much to contribute to the conversation and the transition. Team Moses brings wisdom and experience. Team Joshua brings energy and drive, while Team Rahab brings perspective and hope. In the original outline of Project Nebo within the local church, the sermon series ended here. The goal was to get all three groups to the top of the mountain and see what happens. Just having some clarity around the generational issues that present themselves and the crisis in the American church is a starting point. But now what? Just knowing the challenges better does not in itself solve the problem that the church faces. The church today is stuck and needs an "outside force" to act upon it, to take inspiration from Newton's First Law of Motion. The church needs God.

The Secular Age

Perhaps the best description of the predicament facing the church comes from philosopher and author Charles Taylor, the leading scholar in the field of secularism. In his book, *A Secular Age*, he explores what it means to live in our current secular age, a time when people and even large swaths of the world's societies are increasingly indifferent to religion or reject it altogether. He examines how the role of religion has changed in recent decades and what those changes mean and forecast for the future. One of Taylor's conclusions is that the modern church has been heavily influenced by this drift toward secularism. He even suggests that the church exists and practices theology within a construct he calls the "immanent frame." This means that even in religious circles, most of the conversation is based on a secular reality, and not on the reality of the living God.

When the church faces a challenge, often it assumes that the problem can be solved by simply adding more resources. If only there were more money. If only the church had more staff. If only there were more committed volunteers. This way of thinking is almost impossible to escape. The church has tried, for decades, to solve its problems with the materialistic solutions of secularism.

This drive to solve spiritual problems with secular resources is perfectly illustrated by Walter Brueggemann in his book, *Sabbath as Resistance*. There he talks about Pharaoh's insatiable desire for bricks. It is hard to know why Pharaoh thought that he needed that many bricks. The Hebrew children were forced into an ever-increasing "brick quota," even into making bricks without straw. The Hebrew children were tired of making bricks. However, even after their freedom from slavery, they had trouble escaping a system that called for bricks. Brueggemann termed this a "narrative of scarcity." The Hebrew children sometimes longed to go back to making bricks for pharaoh. When they faced challenges like the need for food and water in the wilderness, they thought about their plight in terms of scarcity. But God had a different plan. God's story for them was a "narrative of abundance." God nourished them with manna from heaven and water from rocks. They had forgotten that the solution to their existential problem could not be solved by the narrative of scarcity or from the immanent frame. Instead, with a challenge like that, they needed to rely on what Taylor labels the "transcendent frame." The church in this time of crisis and transition must find its way to think outside the immanent frame and the narratives of scarcity and into God's transcendence and abundance.

This is the problem with the three Nebo trekking groups. It is good to have them all grouped together at the top of the mountain, but ultimately they are still stuck. When one looks back at the driving scriptural narrative from Deuteronomy, one discovers that there is more to the story. The main actor in the narrative is not Moses, Joshua, or Rahab—but rather is a fourth trekking party on Nebo—the Lord. Furthermore, the trek up Nebo is meaningless unless the Lord goes too.

In the text, God was the One who met Moses at the top of the mountain, and it was God who gave Moses the ability to see the vision for their future. The text says that Moses could miraculously see the entire Promised Land—sights that were not visible to the naked eye. God journeyed up Mount Nebo with Moses and empowered the Israelites to move forward to their future. Team Y-H-W-H is the most important team on Mount Nebo.

And who is this God? The great theologian Robert Jensen taught that God is defined by the way that God has revealed God's self in scripture. Jensen said that "God is whoever raised Jesus from the dead, having before raised Israel from Egypt." God is known by the liberation of Israel from Egypt and the death and resurrection of Jesus. Having this God along on the journey at the pinnacle of Nebo changes everything.

The church in America has many problems. While it has been hemorrhaging members and losing status for decades, the losses have accelerated in the past twenty years. Not only has the church in America seen these dramatic losses across all denominations but also has experienced the pain of infighting and fracturing. The strength and witness of denominations and churches has been diminished. If these trends continue at their current pace, Christianity will evaporate, and many prognosticators out there predict the demise of the church. This was also true during the Revolutionary War when people like Thomas Jefferson predicted that the end of Christianity was just around the corner, and yet the church journeys on.

What the prognosticators then and now are missing is the fourth party on the trek to Mount Nebo. If Teams Moses, Joshua, and Rahab are the only ones traveling up the mountain, their predictions make sense. But the Lord is also on the journey. This is "the God who raised Jesus from the dead, having before raised Israel from Egypt." If this is true, then, despite all evidence to the contrary, the three trekking groups and the church in America can also be raised to new life by this same God.

Holy Mountain

Moses first came to know the Lord in a strange theophany at Mount Sinai. It was there where the Lord spoke to him from a burning bush. What is remarkable about this story is that the Lord does not speak from a mighty sycamore or cedar, but a thorn bush, which was aflame with the fire of God, but not consumed. It was from that bush that God called Moses to his task as a liberator and leader. It was the presence of God that animated the whole journey. In the heart of this call story, Moses asked God for a name to call the Divine. The Lord answered, "I am who I am." It is a circular reference to a Hebrew imperfect verb. It could mean "I will be who I will be," or "I am what I will be," or other tenses of the verb "to be." It is the secret name of God that Moses received, but it is not much of a name at all. It was here that God took the secret name Y-h-w-h. Tradition is to omit the vowels so that God's name is not pronounceable. Originally, the Hebrew language did not have vowels, but over time when vowels were added, they were left out of the name of God so that the reader would not be able to pronounce the sacred name and therefore not be able to take it in vain. This practice is also a recognition of the nature of God. It teaches us that even in our knowing God, there is a lot about God that is unknowable. St. Augustine famously said, "If you can understand, it is not God." The God of Mount Sinai and Mount Nebo cannot be fully understood, only worshiped.

In chapter nine, Mark's Gospel offers us an analogous theophany to the story of Moses and the burning bush. Three disciples journey up a mountain together, but Jesus's presence with them is what changed everything as he was "transfigured" among them. While the story of the transfiguration is set in Galilee, it is clear that this is no ordinary mountain. For one thing, there are no impressive mountains in the Galilee region, just small foothills. This mountain is part of the church's spiritual geography. With Moses and Elijah gathered there, this mountain is or becomes a Sinai. Instead of the burning bush, it is Jesus who burns with the blaze of God and is not consumed. However, this mountain in Galilee also has another spiritual geography—it is also a Nebo. It was there on the Mountain of Transfiguration that Peter, James, and John, like Moses in Deuteronomy, saw the vision of God's future. At Jesus's transfiguration, they were given a glimpse into the future by learning that Jesus would be raised from the dead. This pre-crucifixion revelation of Jesus's glory is meant to give the disciples hope to sustain them through Jesus's suffering and death.

This vision of resurrection is what the church seeks on Mount Nebo. It is a vision not only of the transfiguration of Christ but also of the transfiguration of the church. The church is invited to live into the death and resurrection of Jesus. Project Nebo is a journey of transfiguration based in the glory of the Christ. In the stories of Nebo and Sinai, there is a spiritual geography that is different from the physical geography. Despite the Israelites being miles away from Mount Sinai, where God originally revealed God's nature and name, God again meets them at Mount Nebo. Nebo and Sinai are alpine bookends to the wilderness journey that teaches each generation that the journey to freedom and new life is dependent on God. The Mountain of Transfiguration is located in the same spiritual geography, where God is revealed and the church is transformed. If the church is to be transfigured and resurrected into new life, it will not be because of secular strategies, but because of the presence of the risen Christ.

The church has no life of its own. Its only life is found in resurrection. Too often, followers of Jesus have tried to use human resources and strength to earn eternal life, but all human efforts ultimately lead to death. The church's hope is only in resurrection. The church's strategy is not to adopt a bunch of techniques to be slightly less dead. Rather, the church is called to "Practice Resurrection." Everyone wants to "walk in newness of life" or to have "new and abundant life," but the only way to experience resurrection is to lay down one's life. That is the trouble with resurrection: it requires death. The Hebrew children were delivered from slavery in Egypt not by their own ingenuity or skill but by the power of God. Israel left Egypt not by building boats or using scuba gear. The Lord miraculously parted the sea. Israel overcame Jericho not with catapults and battering rams but by the work of God. At every step of salvation history, it was not the people of God who prevailed but the Lord. As stated before, the only strategy is a Jericho strategy. If the church is going to pass the baton to the next generation, it will not be because of the consultants, experts, techniques, strategies, fundraisers, or buildings. The church has life only in the Lord.

God is God

When Karl Barth, the Swiss theologian realized that all of the modern theology that he had been taught had let him down, he came to the basic, almost nonsensical idea that "God is God." It was this notion—God is God—that broke open his theology and changed everything. This realization is what the church must recover today. Andrew Root sees Barth's theology of a transcendent God as offering a way forward in this secular age:

> When the church can affirm that God is God, its reliance moves from human 'frames, explanations, and structures' and the faculties of the immanent frame to God. "[This] move helps those in the immanent frame find God, because only in confessing that we have no way to find God are we assured that we seek God and not just our own echo.[14]

God is calling the church to a Nebo moment where our only hope is a miracle. While this seems disheartening and dismal from a secular point of view, this is exactly the place where the church needs to be. The church, in so far as it is more than a social club or a human institution, only exists by act of miracle. This has been the core of the church's trouble, living a life dependent on the immanent frame. The trouble with this life is that it is ruled by

14 Pg. 59

natural life cycles of life and death. There are not enough resources and techniques to prevent death. But, the life that God calls the church to live is resurrection life. This life is outside of natural cycles; it is abundant and eternal.

In the United Methodist membership liturgy, the greeting states this strong proclamation: "The Church is of God, and will be preserved to the end of time." The church will find new life because it is not simply a human institution that comes and goes. It is of God and its life comes not from its own strength but from the life of the Holy Trinity. From a human vantage point, there is no case for optimism. But the church does not live on optimism but on hope. And this is not a general hope but a specific hope in Team Y-H-W-H, which consists of the one triune, eternal God, Father, Son, and Holy Spirit.

This book began with Andrew Root's fictional character named Woz, a Millennial who had his struggles with drugs and finding his place. His grandmother was a stabilizing force in his life. When she was dying, she gave him three pearls of wisdom, "Take care of your teeth. Save some money. Go find God." After her death he walked into her aging and declining church and asked for help in finding God. They did not know what to do. It created a crisis, but it also broke them open for the Holy Spirit to work. They realized that their challenge was not that they did not have the resources or the skills to reach new members, but that they needed to find God. The church was no longer "the star of its own story," but in trying to find God, God found them. That is what is at the heart of Project Nebo. God has found us. The church has come to a place where it welcomes God to do God's work in transforming the church for its future. The church is not the star of the story. This is the Lord's church, and the Lord will preserve it and raise it from the dead.

Prayer

God of every high mountain and low valley, you are God of the soaring Mount Nebo and the valley of the shadow of death. We are your people, the sheep of your pasture. Without you, we would be utterly lost. We can only say "wow" when we think of how far you've brought us. We marvel at the way you continue to rescue us from the places we find ourselves when we try to do life our way. Thank you for seeing us through the difficulties we have faced as individuals and as a congregation.

As we continue to travel toward the future you have prepared for us, we ask that you continue to prepare us for that future. Mold us into the people you are calling us to be. Make us ready to inhabit the places where milk and honey are abundant and justice and righteousness flow like an ever flowing stream. And teach us to continue to look to you for everything we need.

As we continue to walk the path you set before us, may we never forget your steadfast love and faithful-

ness. May we never forget to thank and honor those who have passed the baton to us. And may we always look for those who would come after us, to receive from us your good news of salvation in Jesus Christ. Make us ever ready to follow where you lead us, even into the unknown.

In the name of the Father, and of the Son, and of the Holy Spirit. Amen.

SIX

Nebo's Blessing: Moving Forward to the Promise

Numbers 6:24-26

> *"May the Lord bless you and keep you, may the Lord make his face to shine upon you and be gracious unto you, may the Lord lift up his countenance upon you and give you peace."*

The Fourth Turning

The Strauss-Howe Generational Theory would describe the current state of the world as being in the fourth turning, a crisis period that comes every fourth generation for many cycles. The

United States and the American church are deeply troubled. Unfortunately, the theory says that the crisis will continue for several more years, possibly with a dramatic climax that will motivate the world to achieve greater peace and stability, thereby ending the crisis. Then the cycle will begin again with a new order that includes the establishment of strong institutions as was seen in the 1950s in the aftermath of World War II.

According to the generational theory, the core of the pressures that animate the crisis is the difficulty of transitioning culture and leadership from one generation to another. American society is in a major transition. This transition is at the heart of the unprecedented political dysfunction in our country and the struggle in the American church, particularly the chaos in the United Methodist Church. For several decades, the largest generation in American society had been Baby Boomers, but now Millennials are the most substantial segment of the population. Though much has already happened, there is more change and transition to come.

It is important to address this generational transition in a proactive way instead of focusing only on the symptoms. Churches must have more open discussions around generational paradigms including how the Holy Spirit is calling each generation to lead during this crisis period. The best example of a similar "turning" in Holy Scripture is the transition between the liberating generation of Moses and the victorious generation of Joshua. The scripture from the end of Deuteronomy and beginning of Joshua, where the people of God gathered at Mount. Nebo is crucial to understanding the present moment.

The Gospel of Nebo

There are many New Testament expressions of Project Nebo, including two images of Nebo's blessing in the Gospels to offer some final theological grounding. The first and clearest example of Project Nebo in the Gospels is the Great Commission in Matthew 28. There on a holy mountain Jesus blesses the disciples. Matthew's Gospel says, "Now the eleven disciples went to Galilee, to the mountain to which Jesus directed them."

One of the strange inconsistencies of the Bible that has puzzled the literalists is that Luke's Gospel clearly has this final episode of Jesus's ministry occurring on the Mount of Olives, near Jerusalem, which has its own theological significance. But Matthew gives this important scene a setting in Galilee. The evangelist is telling the reader that this is the same theological geography from earlier in his Gospel, the unnamed and unknown Mountain of Transfiguration. There in the same spiritual place, if not physical, Jesus gathers the eleven disciples like Moses gathered the tribes and blessed them. Like Moses on Nebo, Jesus's blessing of the disciples is also a commissioning. As the twelve tribes were to enter the Promised Land, the eleven disciples were to "go therefore and make disciples of all nations, baptizing them in the name of the Father and of the Son and of the Holy Spirit, and teaching them to obey everything that I have commanded you." All through the Gospel of Matthew, Jesus has been a Moses-like figure. That parallel continues even into the last verses of the Gospel. Like the story of Moses, Jesus offers them a blessing, "And remember I am with you always, to the end of the age." This illustrates that Christ is active in Project Nebo as the elder blessing the younger. Jesus calls the church to the theological geography of Nebo to bless and then send each generation of disciples into the world. In this way, we are to Jesus as Joshua was to Moses.

At the same time, the blessing works from the opposite direction. One significant example of the Nebo blessing is Simeon and Anna from the Gospel of Luke. This is one of the least known parts of the Christmas story, where the baby Jesus is presented at the temple. Mary and Joseph journeyed to Jerusalem to present Jesus, following Torah practice. At the temple, what is remembered is not what the priest did in his presentation or Mary's purification. What is remembered is that the holy family ran into some strangers named Simeon and Anna. Simeon's age is not revealed in the text, but what is revealed is that he is so old that he is about to die. Anna was 84, a remarkable feat in the ancient world where life spans were short. A similar image in today's world might be the senior saints in local churches. These faithful members are the backbone of the life of the church, showing up weekly or even daily to find fellowship and offer their gifts to serve. The older members of local churches have wisdom to pass down.

The world might be a much better place if more young people listened to more old people. That is one of the unique things about the church. Church is one of the only places where old and young come together. At church, a young person can become friends with an older person. In the aisle of the sanctuary, in the halls of the Sunday School wing, and around the tables of the fellowship hall, church is a holy place where old and young can have meaningful interactions.

In the encounter between the baby Jesus and these two senior citizens, Anna and Simeon, something holy happened. Mary handed off her baby to a complete stranger. Simeon, the old man, takes the baby in his arms and offers a blessing. In the modern imagination, this is a Lion King moment. Like Rafiki, the old man holds the newborn baby up in the air and presents the child to the world while Anna also comes and dotes on the child. Together, they surround him with love and acceptance, offering a blessing.

God Is Calling on the Church Today

God is calling each disciple to be more like Simeon and Anna. The older humans get, the more likely they are to think they have seen everything and the less likely they are to be surprised by anything. But Anna and Simeon, in their old age, knew that they had something yet to see. They needed to hear something from the young, even if it was just the cry of an infant.

A church growth anecdote says that the seven last words of a church are "we have never done it that way before." But those are not the words from Simeon and Anna. Even though they were old and their eyes were growing dim, they had a clear vision of the future. They were working every day to leave a legacy for those who were to come behind them. They were not rigid in their old age but were open to the future and ready to see what God would do.

In a poem about St. Simeon by the late Presbyterian pastor and poet David Steele, a fictional preacher finds evidence from a Bible scholar that "Old Simeon had become an old codger hanging around the temple all the time pronouncing the same blessing over every child presented there." It is comical to imagine Simeon and Anna with cognitive decline, blessing every baby, not just Jesus. They could have been blessing children all day long, as if each one were the Savior of the world. Of course, the poet was joking. That would ruin the story, or would it? Then the poet surprises us. He states,

> When I read the blessing
> And thought about it,
> I began to wish he was right,
> About Simeon--and those babies.
> And I began thinking about our babies.

> And I wished someone,
> Some Simeon,
> Might hold my grandbabies high--
> And yours--
> The born ones and the not yet
> Proclaiming to them
> With great conviction,
> "You are the saviors of the World!"
> Meaning it so absolutely
> Those young 'uns would live it,
> And love it,
> And make it happen!

What if the church took as its job to find Christ children in the world and to hold them up and bless them? What if Jesus's followers saw every child as a Christ child? What if each Christian honored the Christ in each person? What if each church were that kind of church? What if every church held up all the children that came through its doors and sang a blessing over them?

Blessing for All

What these two stories show is that Christ is both the blesser and the blessed—both Moses and Joshua. Maybe this is what is indicated with the strange Christological title from the Book of Revelation, "I am the Alpha and the Omega, the beginning and the end." The whole Project Nebo is bookended and surrounded by the blessings of Christ coming before and after us. By welcoming the young, the church welcomes the Christ Child in its midst. And by receiving the blessing from elders, the younger are blessed by Jesus. The church must not simply look to pass on the good news or pass Christ to the next generation, but also must look to find Christ there.

The greatest blessing of all is Christ's presence with the church. John Wesley's last words serve as a reminder of the importance of this message. His disciples were gathered around him as he was in his final hours and he blessed them with his dying words, "the Best of all, God is with us." That is what drives Project Nebo forward; the church is surrounded by the presence of God.

Project Nebo ends with the blessing and the knowledge, as Paul tells the church in Philippi (1:6), that "God who began a good work in you will be faithful to complete it." God is not through with the church. God will complete what God started. The Moseses bless the Joshuas as the Joshuas bless the Moseses, they both bless the Rahabs, and the Rahabs bless in return. Everyone receives Nebo's blessing. This blessing flows from the life of the Trinity where each person blesses the others and from that blessing flows the new and abundant life that is the hope of the church.

Project Nebo Closing Litany

Leader: *We have journeyed together these six weeks climbing Mount Nebo.*
People: **We have come to this place to hear from God.**
Leader: *Along the way, we have felt many emotions: fear, hope, wonder, anger, sadness, and joy.*
People: **We have shared and we have listened. We are all, at times, Moses, Joshua, and Rahab.**
Leader: *The journey is far from over.*
People: **Indeed, it has only just begun.**
Leader: *The God who has been faithful these many years will continue to lead us.*
People: **We are bound for the Promised Land!**
Leader: *We will not fear, for God goes before and behind us.*
People: **Our God will never leave us or forsake us.**
All: **Who will come and go with us? We are bound for the Promised Land!**

APPENDIX A

A Case Study: First United Methodist of Pensacola, Florida

As First United Methodist of Pensacola, Florida, journeyed through Project Nebo, the church discovered that God is with them during this crucial time. The church discovered a new hope for the future. When the project began, we heard many people hesitant and defensive about their generation. Walls went up and people were uncomfortable talking about age and duty. Some on Team Moses had concerns that they were not wanted or needed any more and others felt like it would be hard to trust the younger generations with the baton. One person said, "We cannot trust the Millennials to take over; there is no hope." When it came to Team Joshua, they too were unsure about this process. If they participated, would anything change? Would Boomers really welcome them to participate in leadership? Members of the Gen Z generation were particularly standoffish. One said, "This is what always happens—the

Boomers do whatever they want, we have to fix it, and the Millennials get the credit." Our Team Rahab also did not fully understand why we were going through this process, but they were the most excited about the project. They were hopeful about the future of the church and the most ready to move forward.

As we launched the Project Nebo sermon series and classes, we certainly heard reservations and doubts about the path ahead. But the miraculous thing was that as the congregation walked through the crisis the church and world face, it also talked through the wisdom of holy scripture. God showed up and walls started coming down. We heard overwhelming thanks for having this conversation, and all three groups participated deeply and shared from the heart. We heard Moseses say that when they came to the church it was strong and that they wanted to leave it better than they found it. Our older members felt called to help mentor and cultivate younger leaders, and our younger members learned that they are just as much a part of the church as anyone else. They realized that they can participate fully. One group of Millennial women had the epiphany that they could step up immediately and make a difference instead of waiting for permission. We learned that our Rahabs were inviting more people to church than anyone else, and they remain our best evangelists. They look forward to being in church each week and are more committed to our future than many members who have been a part of the church a long time. Senior high youth members realized that they were Moseses called to mentor junior high youth so they are ready to lead.

Perhaps most remarkable was seeing the near unanimity around passing the baton— the good news of Jesus Christ. Our congregation emerged committed to practicing radical hospitality—where everyone is welcomed and included by Christ to find new life. Since Project Nebo concluded, we have seen countless conversations break out about our collective future and how God is calling us to change. These conversations have been holy, and learning from each other, we have grown as individuals and as a congregation. We have found that focusing intentionally on this challenge is a blessing.

At the end of the book of Deuteronomy, the Lord tells Moses to bless the people. That is where we are today at the end of this project. God is calling us to bless each other. The core of any blessing in general and Moses's blessing in Deuteronomy 33 is that God is with us. When the Lord is present, the walls of Jericho fall both external and internal, and the waters of the Red Sea part. God makes a way. When we bless one another, we are reminding ourselves and those around us that God is with us. Like the Israelites looking toward an uncertain future in Canaan, we are proclaiming the Lord's presence as we walk the path ahead.

APPENDIX B

Using Project Nebo in the Local Church Sermon Series

The chapters of this book were adapted from a six-week sermon series of the same name preached at First UMC Pensacola during January and February 2024. Participating churches are encouraged to use this material to adapt their own sermon series around this concept. The original series was preached during the season of Epiphany, ending on Transfiguration Sunday, which has its own mountain theme.

Setting up Discussion Groups

1. Decide on a facilitator who can be present at each of the discussion sessions. (Emily Kincaid was our facilitator. Geoffrey Lentz was present at each session but said very little except a short introduction and opening prayer.)
2. Set dates for Team Moses, Joshua, and Rahab sessions. (We held the sessions concur-

rently with the sermon series. First UMC Pensacola offered two of each type of session to give our members ample opportunity to participate.)
3. Advertise the dates and purpose of the sessions. Ask parishioners to self-select into which group seems to fit them best. (We used existing Sunday School classes who generally fit each category and advertised the dates and locations so others could join the sessions.)
4. During each session, the facilitator should ask a question, write it on a whiteboard or poster paper, then record the answers from the group. Move through the questions as it seems appropriate for the group gathered. Try to portion the time for each question so that everyone gets to speak but each question gets attention.
5. Take a photo of the answers, if on a whiteboard, or collect the poster papers and save them in order to collate the answers for the celebration at the end of the project.

Team Questions

Moses Sessions
1. Name the first or one of the first times you were invited into any type of leadership. Who invited you and what did it feel like?

2. How would you describe the baton, the thing we are passing down from one generation to the next?
3. What advice, based on your experiences, would you give to younger generations about leading the church through challenging times?
4. What are some effective ways you believe older generations can support and encourage emerging leaders in the church?
5. In what ways has your generation influenced the current state of the church, and how do you perceive this influence?
6. What wisdom do you want to pass down to those who come after you?

Joshua Sessions
1. Name the first or one of the first times you were invited into any type of leadership. Who invited you and what did it feel like?
2. What changes do you believe are necessary in the church to remain relevant and impactful in today's society?
3. Considering your unique position in the generational timeline, what leadership styles do you think are most effective for today's church?
4. What vision do you have for the church's future, and how is it similar to and different from past paradigms?

5. What challenges do Millennials face in taking up leadership roles in the church, and how can these be addressed?
6. In what ways can the church innovate to resonate more deeply with your generation and those following?

Rahab Sessions

1. Name the first or one of the first times you were invited into any type of leadership. Who invited you and what did it feel like?
2. What can organizations do to reduce these barriers and create a more level playing field for diverse leaders?
3. What kinds of biases or barriers have you faced as an outsider, and how have you dealt with them?
4. What strategies can be employed to bridge the gap between traditional leaders and outsider-emerging leaders?
5. How can leadership be redefined to better accommodate and benefit from outsider perspectives?
6. How has your experience as an outsider shaped your view of leadership, and what unique insights do you bring to the table?

APPENDIX C

Generational Chart

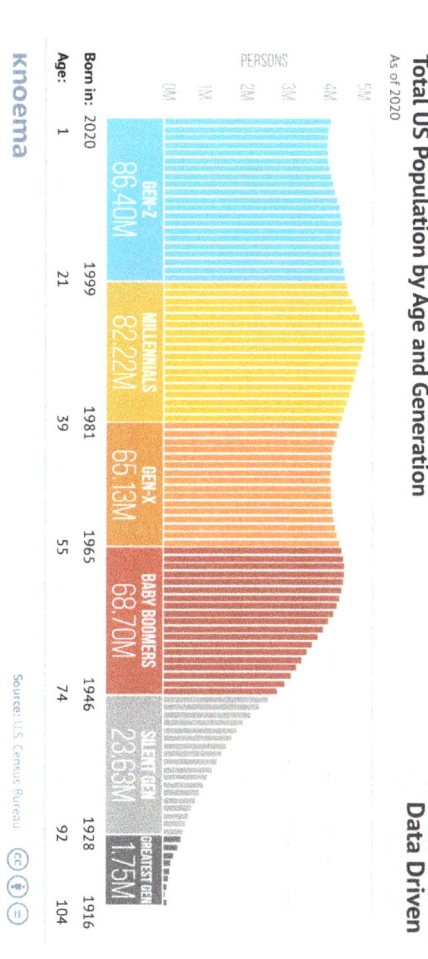

APPENDIX D

Project Nebo Celebration Document

Project Nebo: Celebration
Sunday, February 11 | 10:00 a.m.
First United Methodist Church
of Pensacola, Florida

Over the course of the past six weeks, we have held eight Nebo listening sessions and heard from more than 250 of our parishioners on this topic. There were two Moses sessions, two Joshua sessions, one Rahab session, one session with the leadership of the church, and one session with the youth. We have collected more than 600 responses to the questions, which varied depending on the makeup of the group.

Nebo Generation Groups

Project Nebo, with its focus on generational transition and leadership within the church, has benefited from group discussions that were thoughtfully crafted to address the unique challenges and opportunities each generation faces.

Several key themes emerged from the data and conversations:

THE PROCESS - The vast majority of participants were eager to participate in the conversation and felt that, no matter the "outcome," simply talking about these issues was helpful.

THE BATON - There was great consensus in all sessions around how we define the baton and what it is we want to pass down to the next generation. That consensus centered around the good news of Jesus Christ, the traditions of the church, the trust that God has been leading our church throughout the past 200 years and that God will go with us and lead us into the next 200 years of our church's history.

> Moses - stepping up to identify, recruit, and mentor the next generation
> Joshua - stepping up to take their place in leadership
> Rahab - excitement about what God is doing here and inviting new people

HOSPITALITY - A common theme was the importance of hospitality, inclusion, and welcoming all people into the life of our church. Along with that, the theme of invitation stood out among the responses— inviting new people to church, inviting younger people to the table where decisions are made, inviting new and younger people into the leadership of our church.

COURAGE - "Don't be afraid" is one of the most common themes in scripture. Members recognized this call to have and demonstrate courage as crucial when confronting and accepting changes within the church.

COMMUNITY - A final common theme was the importance of knowing one another and being known in the community of faith. Under this theme, we heard a lot about the need for more small- and medium-sized groups in which people gather for fellowship and faith formation. We also heard a good bit about the need for the "cross-pollination" between groups, including same-aged and intergenerational events and classes or meetings.

Word Clouds

The word clouds were generated from the data gathered at the generation group meetings

1. Challenges

2. Baton

Next Steps:
1. Use the season of Lent as an opportunity to pause and process all the things we've already seen and heard.
2. Continue to have these types of conversations where we look at the bigger picture, gain perspective, and think about who God is calling us to be.
3. Establish new ministry opportunities with and for young millennials and Gen Zs.
    a. New class for young adults
    b. Summer class for college students
4. Formalize mentoring partnerships through confirmation and new leadership opportunities.
5. Renew focus on the baton and passing down the faith.

Bibliography

Alcoba, Natalie. "This Language Was Long Believed Extinct. Then One Man Spoke Up." Reporting from Paraná, Argentina, January 13, 2024.

Brooks, David. *The Second Mountain: The Quest for a Moral life.* (Penguin Books, 2020).

Brueggemann, Walter. Sabbath as Resistance: Saying No to the Culture of Now. (Westminster John Knox Press, 2017).

Davis, Jim, Collin Hansen, Michael Graham, and Ryan P. Burge. *The Great Dechurching: Who's Leaving, Why Are They Going, and What Will It Take to Bring Them Back?* (Zondervan Reflective, 2023).

Howe, Neil, and William Strauss. *The Fourth Turning: An American Prophecy.* (New York: Broadway Books, 1998).

Howe, Neil. *The Fourth Turning Is Here: What the Seasons of History Tell Us about How and When This Crisis Will End.* (Simon & Schuster, 2023).

Jones, Jeffrey M. "U.S. Church Membership Falls Below Majority for First Time." *Gallup News*, March 29, 2021.

King, Martin Luther Jr. "I've Been to the Mountaintop." Audio recording, April 3, 1968, Memphis, Tennessee.

Root, Andrew. *Churches and the Crisis of Decline: A Hopeful, Practical Ecclesiology for a Secular Age.* (Baker Academic, a division of Baker Publishing Group, 2022).

Taylor, Charles. *A Secular Age.* (The Belknap Press, 2007).

About the Authors

Rev. Ashley Davis is an ordained elder in the Alabama-West Florida Conference of the United Methodist Church and a native of Luverne, Alabama. She currently serves as the Director of Connectional Ministries and Assistant to the Bishop, helping to steward the vision of the Annual Conference and align resources with its mission. Ashley was elected as a delegate to the 2024 Southeastern Jurisdictional Conference. She holds a Bachelor of Science from Auburn University and a Master of Divinity from Emory University's Candler School of Theology. Before her current role, she served on staff at Woodland UMC in Pike Road and spent eight years in campus ministry at the Troy University Wesley Foundation. Ashley is a graduate of The Upper Room's Two-Year Academy for Spiritual Formation and is passionate about spiritual renewal, connectional leadership, and missional integrity.

Rev. Emily Kincaid is an ordained deacon in the Alabama-West Florida Conference and serves as the Executive Pastor of First United Methodist Church of Pensacola. She was elected as a delegate to the 2024 General and Jurisdictional Conferences and was chosen to chair the delegation—the first female clergyperson and deacon in the conference to serve in that role. Emily is also a member of the World Methodist Council. She has served as chair of the Board of Ordained Ministry and currently leads as President of the Conference Board of Trustees. A native of Monroeville, Alabama, Emily earned a degree in Cultural and Religious Studies from Huntingdon College and a Master of Divinity with a concentration in Christian Education from Duke Divinity School. Her ministry is centered on collaborative leadership, discipleship formation, and building the Church for the next generation.

Dr. Geoffrey Lentz is an ordained elder in the Alabama-West Florida Conference of the United Methodist Church and serves as the Senior Pastor of First United Methodist Church of Pensacola, Florida. He served as a delegate to the 2024 General Conference and the World Methodist Council. Geoffrey is a native of Pensacola, and holds a Bachelor's degree in Psychology (University of West Florida), Master of Divinity degree (Duke Divinity School), and a Doctorate in Ministry (Drew University). His life mission is to "practice resurrection"—inviting people into new and abundant life in Jesus Christ, renewing the church, bringing hope to the least of these, and growing daily as a disciple of Christ.

About This Book

Project Nebo: Empowering the Generations is a bold and timely guide to navigating generational change in the church. Drawing inspiration from Moses on Mount Nebo—where vision was cast and leadership was passed to a new generation—this book invites churches to embrace the adventure of intergenerational ministry with courage, clarity, and purpose.

Blending theological depth with the sociological insights of Strauss-Howe Generational Theory, the authors offer a compelling vision for how churches can transition leadership, renew congregational life, and foster dynamic partnerships across age groups. With the mountain trekking imagery of "Team Moses," "Team Joshua," and "Team Rahab," Project Nebo maps out the terrain of generational leadership and equips each team to climb together toward a shared future.

More than just theory, Project Nebo is a practical toolkit for transformation. It challenges every generation to take its place in God's ongoing story and build a church that thrives—not in spite of generational differences, but because of them.

Whether you're a pastor, church leader, or curious layperson, this book will give you the theological grounding, sociological framework, and spiritual motivation to lead your church into its next faithful chapter.

www.ingramcontent.com/pod-product-compliance
Lightning Source LLC
Chambersburg PA
CBHW050017090426
42734CB00021B/3305